Influential Leadership

Copyright Notice

Contents

Preface

They say that leaders are born, not made. While it is true that some people are born leaders, some leaders are born in the midst of adversity. Often, simple people who have never had a leadership role will stand up and take the lead when a situation they care about requires it. A simple example is parenting. When a child arrives, many parents discover leadership abilities they never knew existed in order to guide and protect their offspring.

Once you learn the techniques of true Leadership And Influence, you will be able to build the confidence it takes to take the lead. The more experience you have acting as a genuine leader, the easier it will be for you. It is never easy to take the lead, as you will need to make decisions and face challenges, but it can become natural and rewarding.

Influence is subtle, yet incredibly powerful. You can order someone to do a task, but you cannot order them to do their best. It simply does not work and usually has the opposite effect. You can influence people to do their best by providing a strong, motivating example in addition to positive reinforcement. Leadership addresses tasks, while influence addresses attitudes and awareness. Influence is the soul of leadership.

Chapter One:
The Evolution of Leadership

Do not repeat the tactics, which have gained you one victory, but let your methods be regulated by the infinite variety of circumstances.

Sun Tzu

As long as there have been leaders, there have been those who tried to determine how and why they were successful. Leadership itself has not evolved, but our understanding of it has. It is important to understand why very different leadership styles can be effective, why the same leadership techniques will not work in every situation, and which leadership style fits your personality best. Everyone has leadership potential within them, but understanding these concepts will help you maximize your leadership ability.

DEFINING LEADERSHIP

Simply speaking, "leadership" is defined as "the ability to lead." Unfortunately, this is not very helpful. A better definition comes from the BNET online Business Dictionary: *"The capacity to establish direction and to influence and align others toward a common goal, motivating and committing them to action and making them responsible for their performance."* Although this is more descriptive, it is not substantial. It does not tell us what leadership actually *is*, but rather what it *does*.

CHARACTERISTICS OF A LEADER

The mark of a true leader is not a position or title held, but it is how many people are willing to follow them. Santa Clara University and the Tom Peters group outline the following leadership characteristics:

- Honest
- Competent
- Forward-looking
- Inspiring
- Intelligent
- Fair-minded
- Broad-minded
- Courageous
- Straightforward
- Imaginative

LEADERSHIP PRINCIPLES

The United States Army offers 11 Leadership Principles:

- Be tactically and technically proficient
- Know yourself and seek self-improvement
- Know your soldiers and look out for their welfare
- Keep your soldiers informed
- Set the example
- Ensure the task is understood, supervised and accomplished
- Train your soldiers as a team
- Make sound and timely decisions
- Develop a sense of responsibility in your subordinates
- Employ your unit in accordance with its capabilities

- Seek responsibility and take responsibility for your actions

You will notice that none of the above actually tells you *how to lead* in a practical manner. They don't address what to do or say in any given situation. That is because there is no real formula to being a leader. Leadership must come from within and it is based on your personality. In this book, you will learn how to develop your innate leadership abilities and build the confidence required in being a true leader.

A Brief History of Leadership

Historical Leaders

Throughout the centuries, there have been leaders. We are social animals who bond together, but we look for order against the chaos of life. We look to be organized to accomplish tasks as a society that we cannot perform individually. As a result, someone inevitably ends up in charge.

Leaders in the past have generally belonged to one of three categories: Political, Military or Religious.

- Political: Around 1790 B.C., Babylonian ruler Hammurabi created the codified laws, which unified his empire in what was seen as a fair order as all people were subject to the same rules.

- Military: Sun Tzu was a military general in China from 500 B.C. He wrote the Art of War, and although he was a great military leader, his book is actually about how to *not* use armies except as a last resort, focusing more on wise political policies and strategies to prevent war.

- Religious: It may be said that religious leaders have had the greatest impact on their societies, with results that last for centuries.

MODERN LEADERS

With the rise of the industrial revolution, a new kind of leader emerged: Economic. The so-called Captains of Industry found they could build an empire based on modern technology instead of swords. Oil Barons, railroad magnates, and factory owners built large fortunes without the benefit of armies; it was often at the expense of the people they employed. This gave rise to Union leaders and various movements designed to promote justice where abuses were perceived to exist.

The Industrial Revolution also increased the number of Scientific Leaders, as scientists now had easy access to a wide range of new materials for their work. Psychiatry and Psychology came into prominence with studies on the workplace, in regards to improving productivity and the effect on the workforce.

Studies have shown consistently that workers are more productive when they are in a "positive work environment." The attitude and influence of the boss is a major factor in this productivity. If employees feel they are listened to, respected, and treated fairly, they are happier in their work and perform better than those who feel they are disrespected and unappreciated. Which kind of work environment would *you* prefer?

THREE THEORIES OF LEADERSHIP

THE GREAT MAN THEORY

The Great Man Theory was abandoned in favor of the theories of behavioral science. It's easy to be inspired by stories of great men and women who did great things in their lives. Alexander the Great conquered the known world. Genghis Khan then ravaged most of it. Abraham Lincoln freed the slaves. Harriet Tubman saved hundreds from slavery in the Underground Railroad. Mother Theresa aided and comforted thousands in Calcutta who were abandoned by society. Theory goes that these people did great things because they were simply great people determined by fate and fulfilling their destiny.

THE TRAIT THEORY

It has often been said, *"Great leaders are born, not made."* Trait Theory takes this saying literally. If you have the ability to lead, you were born with it, with no way to learning those skills. This theory expands on the Great Man Theory by defining what makes great leaders "great."

Today, we recognize that true leadership seems to come from a combination of both theories – and more. As we have seen, there are wide varieties of leadership qualities. Everyone has some ability in at least one or more of these areas. This means that under the right circumstances, anyone can rise to a leadership role and be successful based on the leadership style that best matches their personality if they know how to use that ability to properly address the situation at hand. Other leadership skills can indeed be learned, developed, and mastered.

TRANSFORMATIONAL LEADERSHIP

In 1978, James MacGregor Burns introduced the idea of transformational leadership as he researched political leaders. Burns theorized that "transformational leadership" is actually a process where leaders interact with their followers and inspire each other to advance together. His characteristics and behaviors demonstrated the differences between "management" and "leadership." People and organizations are transformed due to the leadership style and abilities of the leader, who is able to convey a vision and guide the transformation.

Bernard M. Bass, in 1985, added to Burns' transformational leadership theory buy shifting the focus to the followers. It is not the individual traits and vision of the leader that matter as much as it is their ability to influence the feelings, attitudes, and commitment of their followers. As we mentioned before in productivity studies, if followers feel they can trust a leader (or better yet, if they admire a leader who can stimulate a sense of loyalty and respect) the followers go beyond what was originally expected of them and will do so happily. As a result, productivity and unity increases. The followers are transformed by a charismatic, motivational leader.

SUMMARY

Through all of the studies, we have seen that there are a variety of attributes and abilities associated with leadership, and these vary from leader to leader. Some leaders are great orators, others great writers. Some leaders are very quiet, but the force of their logic or passion wins the day. The difference between a good leader and a great leader is partly the number of leadership skills they have developed. The other part is their ability to apply those skills properly to those who would follow. We will address these issues in the next section.

PRACTICAL ILLUSTRATION

Julie and Mindy had worked side by side for over five years. They chatted between projects and took lunch breaks together. When the company restructured, Julie was given a management position and Mindy became her subordinate. Mindy felt that it was unfair that she now had to take instructions from Julie and her negative attitude caused the department to lose productivity. Julie understood that it would take time to earn back Mindy's respect. She kept a positive attitude when working with Mindy and always kept Mindy informed of things that were relevant to Mindy's job. She assigned tasks to Mindy that she knew Mindy could accomplish and she gave appropriate feedback when work was delivered. Julie took responsibility for her decisions and didn't blame others when things went wrong. Over time, she gained Mindy's respect and the department's productivity soared.

Chapter Two:
Situational Leadership

You manage things; you lead people.
Murray Hopper

Now we get to the nuts and bolts of leadership. The definitive leadership style research comes from Paul Hersey and Kenneth Blanchard, which they expressed in their Situational Leadership Model. The Hersey-Blanchard model addresses the key to practical leadership development: the attributes and styles of the *followers*.

Not everyone is on the same intellectual, maturity, compliance, or motivational level. Different people are motivated by different things, and this must be taken into account if one is to be a great leader. Communications experts consider it critical to tailor your message to your "target audience." It is the followers that you want to motivate and influence and you cannot do that if you don't know whom you are trying to motivate or influence.

The Situational Leadership model addresses four types of leadership styles, based on the follower:

- Telling
- Selling
- Participating
- Delegating

The goal is to develop followers to the Delegating level as seen below:

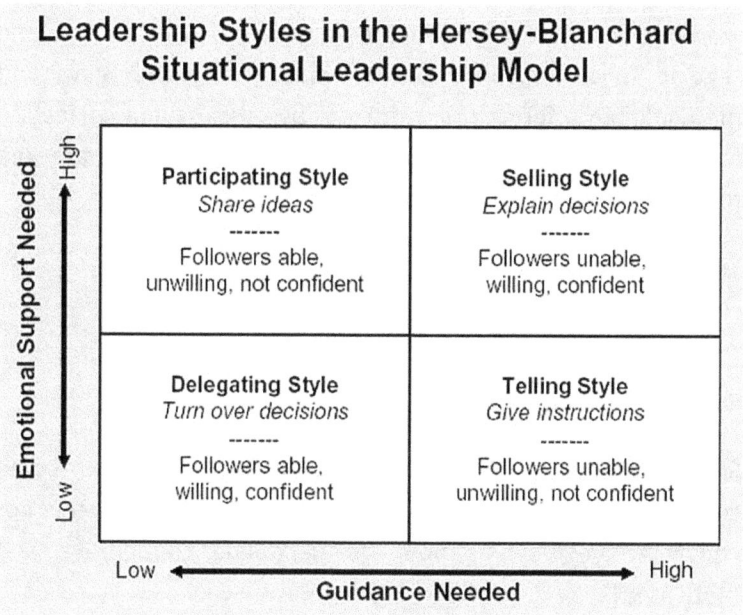

Leadership Styles in the Hersey-Blanchard Situational Leadership Model

	Low ← Guidance Needed → High	
High Emotional Support Needed **Low**	**Participating Style** *Share ideas* ------- Followers able, unwilling, not confident	**Selling Style** *Explain decisions* ------- Followers unable, willing, confident
	Delegating Style *Turn over decisions* ------- Followers able, willing, confident	**Telling Style** *Give instructions* ------- Followers unable, unwilling, not confident

SITUATIONAL LEADERSHIP: TELLING

Telling is the lowest level of leadership style. Most new employees require direct instructions, so this is called the "Telling" or "Directing" style. The follower is characterized by low competence and high commitment, being unable to comply, with possible feelings of insecurity.

The leader must focus highly on tasks, rather than a relationship with the employee, as a relationship does not yet exist.

When an employee can't do the job because they are unknowledgeable, the leader must spend much more time working with the employee, offering clear instructions and regular follow up. The leader must be encouraging and motivational, offering praise for positive results and correction for less than positive results. The idea is to motivate the follower to rise to the next level of ability.

This is a very leader-driven stage.

SITUATIONAL LEADERSHIP: SELLING

Selling addresses the follower who has developed some competence with an improved commitment. The follower is not convinced yet, but is open to becoming cooperative and motivated.

The leader must still focus highly on tasks and this still requires much of the leader's time, but the focus now also includes developing a relationship with the employee. Build upon the trust that has begun to develop and the encouragement that has been demonstrated. The leader must spend more time listening and offering advice, scheduling the follower for additional training if the situation requires it.

The goal is to engage the follower so they can develop to the next level. There is less "telling" and more "suggesting" which leads to more encouragement, acting as a coach. It is recognition that they have progressed and motivates them to progress even further.

This is a very leader-driven stage.

SITUATIONAL LEADERSHIP: PARTICIPATING

Participating addresses the follower who is now competent at the job, but remains somewhat inconsistent and is not yet fully committed. The follower may be uncooperative or performing as little work as possible, despite their competence with the tasks

The leader must participate with and support the follower. The leader no longer needs to give detailed instructions and follow up as often, but does need to continue working with the follower to ensure the work is being done at the level required.

The follower is now highly competent, but is not yet convinced in his or her ability or not fully committed to do their best and excel. The leader must now focus less on the tasks assigned and more on the relationship between the follower, the leader, and the group.

This is a very follower-driven, relationship-focused stage.

SITUATIONAL LEADERSHIP: DELEGATING

Delegating is the ultimate goal: a follower who feels fully empowered and competent enough to take the ball and run with it, with minimal supervision. The follower is highly competent, highly committed, motivated, and empowered.

The leader can now delegate tasks to the follower and observe with minimal follow up, knowing that acceptable or even excellent results will be achieved. There is a low focus on tasks and a low focus on relationships. There is no need to compliment the follower on every task, although continued praise for outstanding performance must be given as appropriate.

This is a very follower-driven stage.

PRACTICAL ILLUSTRATION

Jackie became frustrated with her staff members. She said to her manager, "I feel like I'm putting in 120%. I'm exhausted!"

Paulette frowned a little. "Whenever I hear that, I feel like perhaps the leader is working so hard because they are doing things that might be the jobs of the followers."

Jackie admitted, "I give a lot of detailed information and follow up with my employees very frequently, just to make sure everything goes perfectly."

Paulette was honest with her. "While it's great that you're so attentive, perhaps your staff is feeling micromanaged. Even if you're afraid that something might go awry, if you step back to let them to carry out tasks on their own, you may ultimately see better results."

Jackie took Paulette's advice. When she trusted her employees, things went much more smoothly.

Chapter Three:
A Personal Inventory

Courage - not complacency - is our need today.
Leadership not salesmanship.
John F. Kennedy

In 2002, Jossey Bass published a book by James Kouzes and Barry Posner called *The Leadership Challenge (Copyright © 2000-2012 by John Wiley & Sons Canada, Ltd, or related companies. All rights reserved.)* Building upon the Hersey-Blanchard model and other transformational leadership models, they went to the heart of what skills are required by the leader to stimulate such a transformation. What abilities are able to influence followers and bring them to accept the leader's vision as their own?

AN INTRODUCTION TO KOUZES AND POSNER

James Kouzes and Barry Posner asked thousands of people to rank list of characteristics associated with leadership, including the seven top qualities that motivated them to follow willingly. They gave this survey to over 75,000 people over a 20-year period.

In their book, *The Leadership Challenge (Copyright © 2000-2012 by John Wiley & Sons Canada, Ltd, or related companies. All rights reserved.)* the authors identified five abilities that were crucial to successful leadership:

- **Model the Way**: You must lead by example. You can't come into work 10 minutes late every day if you want your employees to arrive on time.

- **Inspire a Shared Vision**: If you capture the imagination, you will inspire creative thought and increase loyalty. The vision doesn't need to be grandiose, but it needs to be communicated effectively for others to adopt it as one of their own.

- **Challenge the Process**: Don't continue doing something just because "We've always done it that way." Situations change, and sometimes a policy or procedure never worked well in the first place. Think outside the box.

- **Enable Others to Act**: Truly empower people to act on their own within their level of authority. The famed Ritz-Carlton hotel empowers every employee at all levels to spend up to $1000 on behalf of a guest (who is informed reimbursement will be required for whatever request they make).

- **Encourage the Heart**: A positive attitude is infectious. If the leader appears passionate or excited about the vision, others will catch the enthusiasm as well.

A PERSONAL INVENTORY

The results of the Kouzes/Posner study, with the most important quality at the top:

- Honest
- Forward-looking
- Competent
- Inspiring
- Intelligent
- Fair-minded
- Broad-minded
- Supportive
- Straightforward
- Dependable
- Cooperative
- Determined
- Imaginative
- Ambitious
- Courageous
- Caring
- Mature
- Loyal
- Self-controlled
- Independent

CREATING AN ACTION PLAN

Now that you understand the various concepts, it's time to plan how to put them into action by incorporating them into your life.

Set Leadership Goals: In leadership, as in life, you will never come to the end of your learning, but you want to rank in priority order those qualities you want to develop.

Address the Goals: Determine how you will accomplish your goals. Do you feel you need to learn more about teamwork so you can better lead a team? Join a team sport. Do you want to communicate better? Take a creative writing class or join Toastmasters and get some public speaking experience. Toastmasters are also great if you are shy and want to feel more comfortable in social situations.

Seek Inspiration: Learn about a variety of leaders, including their styles in dealing with challenges. Read books and conduct research on the internet or at libraries.

Choose a Role Model: Based on your research, choose a role model that fits your personality. You might choose a dynamic leader like Teddy Roosevelt, or an intellectual leader like Albert Schweitzer or Albert Einstein. Read several biographies and find videos on his or her life.

Seek Experience: Take a leadership role on a social group or club. Gain experience working with people on many levels.

Create a Personal Mission Statement: Imagine your legacy. How do you want to be remembered? What do you want people to think of you? What type of leader you determined to be? Write a statement that defines who you will become.

PRACTICAL ILLUSTRATION

Yolanda wasn't sure why the moral of her employees was down. She'd modeled the way. She had communicated their shared vision Yolanda had made changes and fostered a workplace where ingenuity was rewarded. She definitely worked on enabling others to act, in order to have her employees exert their authority. It was only when she went back to her training manual on Leadership that she realized what she'd been missing.

Yolanda entered into the meeting room with a new, more positive attitude. She started by showing enthusiasm and passion for their tasks at hand. She made sure to smile during the meeting, and while of course she had to be an authority figure, when it was realistic, she found ways to genuinely compliment others to show them that their work was appreciated. It was clear that the manual was right. 'A positive attitude is infectious.'

Chapter Four:
Modeling the Way

Some look at things that are, and ask why. I dream of things
that never were and ask why not?
George Bernard Shaw

Remember that the best leaders are examples of what they want their followers to be. George Washington rode into battle with his troops. You cannot lead from the rear, and sending your followers out to take the heat and face the challenges while you remain in an ivory tower will eliminate any possibility of respect.

By definition, a leader is in the *lead*, right up front, ready to take the heat if something goes wrong. If something does go wrong, a true leader never blames his followers even if in fact they failed. A true leader takes the blame, and then addresses how to correct the problems that arose.

DETERMINING YOUR WAY

Once you have chosen your role model, study what qualities made them successful. Learn about what challenges they faced and how the challenges were met. Learn about the ideas and philosophies that drove them and made them successful. Study again the Hersey- Blanchard model and see how different situations called for different styles of leadership.

Since there is no leader in history who has not had failures, pay particular attention to how your hero deals with adversity. George Washington nearly lost the American Revolution through major hesitations in leadership and in fact, he lost New York to the British general William Howe, but he learned from his mistakes and the rest, as they say, is history.

BEING AN INSPIRATIONAL ROLE MODEL

Leadership is neither for the timid nor for the arrogant. Confidence is often resented or misinterpreted for arrogance. People who lack self-confidence often feel intimidated by a true leader. This should never hold you back. If you have honesty, integrity and deal with everyone fairly, then others will see that. Be willing to listen to criticism, but also consider the source. If you are too afraid of what others might say about you, or you ignore legitimate complaints insisting on respect solely because of your position, you will lose the respect and cooperation of your followers and peers.

President Theodore Roosevelt said it best:

"It is not the critic who counts; not the man who points out how the strong man stumbles, or where the doer of deeds could have done them better. The credit belongs to the man who is actually in the arena, whose face is marred by dust and sweat and blood, who strives valiantly; who errs and comes short again and again; because there is not effort without error and shortcomings; but who does actually strive to do the deed; who knows the great enthusiasm, the great devotion, who spends himself in a worthy cause, who at the best knows in the end the triumph of high achievement and who at the worst, if he fails, at least he fails while daring greatly. So that his place shall never be with those cold and timid souls who know neither victory nor defeat."

INFLUENCING OTHERS' PERSPECTIVES

You may have heard that perception is reality. You must always present an honest, caring, dedicated attitude to inspire others. To inspire loyalty, you must have a track record of honesty and fairness. If any of your followers do feel they have been wronged, for whatever reason, you need to address the issue immediately. People talk, and a problem ignored is a problem that grows.

Believe it or not, the most powerful influence you can have is often not trying to influence someone. When people believe you are open to their suggestions and believe they have been heard, they will work harder even if they disagree with the methods or goals. That is the power of listening. Simply listening to others makes them feel empowered, even if you don't accept their suggestions. If a follower feels there's no point talking to you, they won't, and they will disengage themselves from your vision and will only follow your directions begrudgingly.

If you are seen as going the extra mile, your followers are more likely to go the extra mile. If you hide in your office and people never see you, you will be perceived as out of the loop, uninformed, uninterested, and therefore unworthy to lead. Many a successful corporate executive makes it a point to be seen by their employees every day. If an employee is to be commended for something, it is done publicly, often right in the middle of their workplace while they are surrounded by their coworkers. That sends a powerful message to everyone.

PRACTICAL ILLUSTRATION

Justin had a difficult time being a leader lately. Things had just felt monotonous and stale, and he was wondering why he'd ever wanted to be a leader in the first place. He sat down to talk with the leader of another group of employees to refocus.

Amy listened to Justin, and then she asked him, "In the past, when you dreamed about becoming a leader, what other leaders inspired you?"

Justin thought about this for a moment, and then he said, "I've always been inspired by Martin Luther King, Jr. He was powerful and peaceful at the same time. He was courageous, and he stood up for his beliefs."

Amy smiled. "How can you use his example to inspire and influence your followers?"

This got Justin thinking, and before he knew it, he had a list of ideas for how he could reinvigorate his staff and himself.

Chapter Five:
Inspiring a Shared Vision

I suppose leadership at one time meant muscles; but today it means getting along with people.
Mohandas K. Gandhi

The key to true leadership is to inspire a shared vision among your followers. Before you can convey a vision, however, you have to develop it. You must be clear in your vision, live it before others can see it, and model it from your behavior.

CHOOSING YOUR VISION

What do you want to accomplish, and what do you need to do to get there? Determine attainable goals and focus on them. King Arthur sought the Holy Grail. Lewis and Clark mapped much of the United States. NASA took us to the moon. What is your vision?

Your vision will provide a sense of direction for you and your followers. In the military, focus is on "the mission." Whatever the mission is, everyone is dedicated to it. Let your vision be like a lighthouse on a hill, guiding ships to safety and warning them away from the rocks.

COMMUNICATING YOUR VISION

Communication is more than just the words you say or the memos you write. Remember, actions speak louder than words. Take every opportunity to communicate your vision in words and deeds. One of the best ways to communicate a vision is to sum it up in a simple catch phrase.

Post your slogan, catch phrase and mission statement in prominent locations. When you send out emails, list it in quotes below your signature block. Hold meetings occasionally or hand out "Visionary Awards" to people who exemplify your vision. Above all, lead by example.

IDENTIFYING THE BENEFIT FOR OTHERS

Answer the question, "What's in it for me?" as if you were one of your own followers. The answer might not always be obvious. Certainly, performance bonuses and awards work, but most followers enjoy being part of a larger, successful organization. Everyone loves a winner. When the home team wins at the stadium, you would think the fans in the stand were the players by the way they share in the victory and excitement.

We are social creatures who like to feel like we belong. We crave acceptance. If you can get your followers to accept your vision as their own, and excite them about being part of it, they will often excel beyond what you (or they) thought possible. Be sure to reward loyalty and performance above and beyond the call of duty.

PRACTICAL ILLUSTRATION

Bruce spoke passionately about his company's vision. He believed in their product, and he wanted his employees to feel the same enthusiasm. He'd been wracking his brain for a way to instill this in his followers as their leader. One day, the answer came to him.

He got nice paper and printed out certificates. He also bought small prizes, like candies, brightly colored office supplies, and lottery tickets. He waited until Sean, one of his newer employees, used his own enthusiasm and passion to secure a new client.

Bruce announced to the office. "I'd just like to take a moment to congratulate Sean on his new client. He used his enthusiasm for our product to sign them on. I'd like to give him this Visionary Award for exemplifying our vision."

Bruce continued to give out these awards, inspiring his employees to become excited about their vision.

Chapter Six:
Challenging the Process

Leadership: the art of getting someone else to do something you want done because he wants to do it.

Dwight D. Eisenhower

Far too often, we cling to what is familiar, even if what we cling to is known to be inadequate. Most large groups are governed by the law of inertia: if it takes effort to change something, nothing will change. As a leader, you must search out opportunities to change, grow, innovate, and improve.

There is no reward without risk however, so you must be willing to experiment, take risks, and learn from any mistakes. Ask questions, even if you fear the answers. Start with the question, "Why?" Why are things the way they are? Why do we do things the way we do?

THINK OUTSIDE THE BOX

A *paradigm* is an established model or structure. Sometimes they work quite well, but often they are inadequate or even counterproductive. Sometimes it is necessary to "think outside the box" and break the paradigm. Don't be afraid to ask the question "Why?" Ask questions of your followers, employees, customers, former leaders. Answers and ideas can be found in the least likely places. Often the lowest ranking persons in an organization can tell you exactly what is wrong because they see it daily from their vantage points.

DEVELOPING YOUR INNER INNOVATOR

Innovation is more than just improvement on a process or procedure; it is a total redirection or restructuring based upon stated goals and research. While it can be helpful to adapt an outdated procedure or task to today's standards, often the procedure itself is the problem, not the manner in which it is implemented. Innovators reverse engineer policies and procedures based on the new vision and goals, working from the target backwards, rather than from the status quo looking forward.

To be sure, not all innovative strategies will be feasible or cost effective. Requiring an entirely new computerized network and infrastructure, for example, may cost hundreds of thousands of dollars and produce little improved efficiency over the old one. However, if you don't start thinking "outside the box," you will miss many valuable solutions that can and will work.

Note that change should never be made simply for the sake of change. Change can be exciting, but it can also be unnerving and difficult for employees. Constant change causes frustration.

Moreover, if you seem to change too many things too often, you will lose respect, as your followers perceive you don't really know what you are doing, so be sure to plan your innovations carefully. There should be solid evidence that a new way of doing things is likely to work before you invest money and everyone's time.

Keep focused on the goals and be willing to break the rules if they need to be broken. Just make sure they really need to be broken and you don't break something that needs to keep working! With proper research and planning, you can dare to be bold!

SEEING ROOM FOR IMPROVEMENT

A strong vision does not lend itself to mediocrity. A drive to excellence always seeks improvement. If you accept 95% efficiency as a goal, the efficiency will inevitably slip to 90%. If that's considered "good enough," it will become hard to keep it above 85% and so on. A vision is a goal that is strived to achieve.

Goals must not be unrealistic or unattainable, or the followers will simply give up trying altogether, becoming dispirited and demoralized in the process. If 95% of people fail to meet a standard, then that standard is likely too high and must be changed. On the other hand, the bar must not be set so low that little or no effort is required to meet it.

Based on your vision, set high goals that are attainable but with some degree of difficulty, and reward those who meet the goals. If a large number of followers are meeting the goal, raise the target. If only a very few are meeting it, lower it somewhat.

Investigate any potential bottlenecks that might be stifling progress and resolve them. Talk to your followers about possible solutions. The people who actually do the work are far more likely to be able to tell you why they are having difficulty accomplishing a task than their supervisors.

LOBBYING FOR CHANGE

To lobby for change, you need to influence people and excite them to your vision. You may need to persuade a reluctant boss or fight a corporate culture that doesn't understand what you are trying to do. In that case, you need to demonstrate why your requested change needs to occur.

Do your research, and always enter a meeting by being prepared. Study the situation and present all of your findings in a short report, preferably with simple charts or graphs. Give them something they can easily understand. Have the details ready in case you are asked a question, but don't overload people with facts. Show as clearly as possible how your plan will effect positive change.

If you are lobbying your own followers, the same is true. You may want to revolutionize a cultural change. Perhaps you are a shop manager and people are unmotivated. You may need to bring about change slowly, rather than with one big dramatic gesture. On the other hand, you may need to shake things up in a big way. Whatever the situation, you can successfully lobby for change if you attack the problem with a plan, sound reasoning, and infectious enthusiasm!

PRACTICAL ILLUSTRATION

David entered into his leader's office. Kaitlyn welcomed him inside, and the two of them sat down. David asked, "I was wondering why you wanted to see me. I hope nothing's wrong."

Kaitlyn said, "Absolutely not. Things are going wonderfully. You met your sales goals for this quarter, and as a whole, we're meeting the goals we set."

David nodded, not understanding why he'd been called to her office.

Kaitlyn said. "The best time to plan for the future is when things are going well. We need to plan our next step. Now that we've met this goal, we need to challenge ourselves with another one. I called you here today so that you could help make a measurable, attainable goal for our team."

David was more than happy to pitch in and give his input. This helped Kaitlyn build a relationship with her employee, and challenging them with another goal also set an example for her staff, too.

Chapter Seven:
Enabling Others to Act

The only man who makes no mistakes is the
man who never does anything.
Theodore Roosevelt

As mentioned before, you cannot do your followers' work for them. Besides, if you do their work, what are they getting paid for? You have your own work to do. This is the ultimate goal of the Hersey-Blanchard situational Leadership model: to develop your followers to the point where you can delegate tasks without a lot of oversight.

To be a true leader, you must enable others to act responsibly and not encourage bad worker habits by compensating for them or overlooking them. At the same time, you cannot berate a follower for trying hard but making an honest mistake. The goal of a leader is to empower others to work. To the extent that you can do this is the extent that you will be successful.

ENCOURAGING GROWTH IN OTHERS

A positive attitude is essential to encouragement. No one likes to fail and many take it very personally. While failure should never be rewarded, an understanding attitude and positive outlook can work wonders. A child only learns to walk by falling down many times. The focus is not on the fall, but on getting up. The goal is to walk...then to run.

Meeting with an employee one-on-one is important to positive motivation. Here again, you must use the power of listening. Avoid blame when something goes wrong and focus on the reason for the failure. You may learn someone needs more training, more self-confidence, or more freedom. You may learn someone does not have the tools needed to be successful. You will never know if you don't ask questions and listen – or worse, if you berate someone for a failure.

If someone is willfully defiant, then feel free to be stern and resolute. Take disciplinary action if necessary and document the conversation. If you allow someone to be defiant or lazy out of a misplaced concern for his or her feelings, you will be performing a great injustice against the rest who are working hard. In most cases, people really do want to do a good job and they have a sense of pride when they meet a challenge.

CREATING MUTUAL RESPECT

You will never be worthy of respect if you don't give respect. Respect should be given to everyone at all levels unless they deliberately do something to lose that respect.

You need to build respect in other ways as well. Be visible to your followers. Show them you are available and interested in knowing everything about what they do. Develop and demonstrate your knowledge of the organization and details of the product, service, or operation. If you are perceived as being knowledgeable and can answer questions, you will not only earn respect, but will motivate others to learn as well.

THE IMPORTANCE OF TRUST

Respect inevitably leads to trust. Do what you say and say what you mean. Under-promise and over-deliver can help manage expectations. If you are given a task you know will take you one hour, say you "should" have it done in two hours. You never know when you'll get a phone call that eats into your time or when an emergency may pop up. If you get done in less than two hours, you will be perceived as a hero. If not, you can call and apologize that it will be "a little later" without much trouble because you said you *should* have it done. You didn't promise that you *would* have it done. If people feel they can rely on you, they will trust you.

Also let people know that you are not asking them to do anything you would not do yourself, or have done in the past. Work hard and be seen working hard. If you come in early and see others who are there early as well, stop by and simply mention that fact positively. A simple word of recognition will go a long way to earning respect. Without respect, you will never have loyalty and without loyalty, you cannot trust your followers. Without mutual trust and respect, you cannot accomplish great things.

Remember: while your people need to be able to trust you, you need to build them up to the level where you can also trust them.

PRACTICAL ILLUSTRATION

Adam worked on building respect with his staff from the beginning. He came back from lunch, and he waved to one of his followers, Catherine. He stopped by her cubicle and asked her, "How are things going?"

Catherine sighed and said, "I've been trying to be innovative about this next product launch like you said, but I'm really struggling with finding a new angle."

Adam said, "Is that the same one due by the end of the week?"

"Yes. Do you think you could get me some help with brainstorming?"

Adam assigned another follower to partner with Catherine that he knew excelled at fresh ideas and innovation. Because he showed respect to his followers, they trusted him to let them know how projects were going, good or bad. The problem was addressed in a quick and effective manner.

Chapter Eight:
Encouraging the Heart

Those who fail to plan, plan to fail.
Anonymous

One of the worst developments in the workplace was the creation of the term "Human Resources." Formerly known as the "Personnel Department," the focus was on dealing with people as *persons*. At a time when industry was supposedly focused on making the workplace more humane in order to increase job satisfaction and productivity, it took a major step backwards.

No one wants to be considered a "human resource." A resource is something you use as long as it is functional. When the shelf life expires or is no longer as effective as it once was, you throw it away without a thought. It would be a glorious thing if every Human Resource department was abolished and the name Personnel made resurgence.

Employees, workers and followers are not robots. Human beings have intellect and emotions. Failing to deal with them on those levels will ultimately backfire. You cannot program loyalty.

SHARING REWARDS

If your followers are going to share in the work, make certain they share in the rewards. If you are going to get a bonus for a successful task, share at least a portion of it with your followers. More than one employee has felt betrayed by leadership when the boss gets a big bonus and those who do all the work get nothing. You don't need to give them half or divide it all up among all your followers, but you should at least throw them a party, provide a free lunch, or give everyone a pair of movie tickets or a lottery ticket. Do something to show they didn't work hard only to see you take all the credit.

CELEBRATING ACCOMPLISHMENTS

Set both personal and team goals and milestones. Nothing motivates someone like public recognition. Although some may seem somewhat embarrassed by a public display, inside they are proud they have been recognized. There has never been a recorded study that quotes an employee who was honored in public with them saying that they never wanted that to happen again. Celebrate team milestones as well. It breaks up the routine of the workday, gives a well-deserved break, and motivates people to work harder when they return to work refreshed.

MAKING CELEBRATION PART OF YOUR CULTURE

You don't need to decorate the office each day or have morning pep rallies, but the workplace should never be dreaded by employees. People spend most of their waking lives at work, with substantially less time for family, friends and activities they would much rather be doing. By the very definition, they come to "work" and you have to pay them to be there. People have to feel motivated by more than just a paycheck.

Be sure to have a welcoming environment where people feel respected. Celebrate special occasions to break up the routine, but don't make celebration itself the routine of no work will get done.

PRACTICAL ILLUSTRATION

Eric's team worked all quarter, sometimes pulling late nights, to meet all their metrics and goals. Eric's supervisors saw this, and they rewarded him with a bonus for a job well done as a leader. Eric was proud of himself, but he was equally proud of his staff. While it wasn't necessarily to split the bonus with all his employees, he did come up with a way to reward them for their hard work.

Eric called his team together and said, "I'd like to announce that this quarter we didn't just meet our goals. We exceeded them! Because we all did such a fantastic job, I'm having lunch catered on Friday by our favorite place. Don't bring lunch from home. Just bring your appetites!"

Eric made sure not to plan anything pressing or important that day so that his employees could celebrate and enjoy a job well done.

Chapter Nine:
Basic Influencing Skills

The country is full of good coaches. What it takes to win is a
bunch of interested players.
Don Coryell

The best leaders are able to influence others to do something
and think it was all their idea. Don't worry about taking credit
for every good thing that happens on your watch. As the leader,
you get credit whenever your followers succeed because you
created the environment that allowed their success.

THE ART OF PERSUASION

Aristotle was a master of the art persuasion, and he outlines his
thinking in his work, Rhetoric, where he identifies three
important factors: ethos, pathos, and logos.

- **Ethos** (credibility) persuades people using character. If
  you are respectful and honest, people will be more
  likely to follow you because of your character. Your
  character convinces the follower that you are someone
  who is worth listening to for advice.

- **Pathos** (emotional) persuades people by appealing to
  their emotions. For example, when a politician wants to
  gain support for the bill, it inevitably is argued, "it's for
  the children!" Babies, puppies, and kitties abound in
  advertising for a reason. Although a car is neither male
  nor female, they are sometimes called "sexy" in car

commercials. Pathos allows you to tie into emotional triggers that will capture a person's attention and enlist their support, but it can be easily abused, leading to a loss of Ethos, as described above.

- **Logos** (logical) persuades people by means persuading by appealing to their intellect. This was Aristotle's favorite and his forte', but not everyone reacts on a rational level.

Of the three, Ethos must always come first. Ideally, you want to appeal to Pathos, back your arguments up with Logos, and never lose Ethos. President Bill Clinton appealed to people using Pathos, saying often, "I feel your pain," but there were serious questions raised about his Ethos, and he often did not back up his appeals with Logos. There is no doubt that he was a successful, but there is also no doubt that he was not as successful as he could have been.

THE PRINCIPLES OF INFLUENCE

Robert B. Cialdini, Ph. D. once said, "It is through the influence process that we generate and manage change." In his studies, he outlined five universal principles of influence, which are useful and effective in a wide range of circumstances.

Reciprocation: People are more willing to do something for you if you have already done something for them first. Married couples do this all the time, giving in on little things so they can ask for that big night out or a chance to watch the game later.

Commitment: You cannot get people to commit to you or your vision if they don't see your commitment. Once you provide a solid, consistent example, they will feel they have to do the same.

Authority: If people believe you know what you are talking about and accept your expertise, they are far more likely to follow you. Despite the rebel cry, "Question Authority," when people need help with something, they will seek out an authority figure. If you place a man in a tie next to a man in jeans and a ratty T-shirt, people will invariably ask the man in the tie for advice on a technical subject first simply because he *looks* like an authority.

Social Validation: As independent as we like to consider ourselves, we love to be part of a crowd. It will always be a part of us, that school age desire to be accepted, no matter how many times our parents tell us, "If everyone jumped off a cliff, would you join them?" People will always jump on a bandwagon if their friends like the band.

Friendship: People listen to their friends. If they know you and like you, they are far more likely to support you. A pleasant personality can make up for a multitude of failures. More than one leader has been abandoned at the first sign of trouble because they were not very well liked.

CREATING AN IMPACT

As mentioned before, communication is accomplished with more than just words. The more of the previous leadership skills you develop, the more you will make an impact. In addition, the bigger the impact, the greater the positive change you can create.

Impact is created by a number of intangible factors:

- A confident bearing, tempered by a kindly manner

- A strong sense of justice, tempered by mercy

- A strong intellect, tempered by the willingness to learn

- A strong sense of emotion, tempered by self-control

- A strong ability to communicate, tempered by the ability to listen

- A strong insistence on following the rules, tempered by flexibility

- A strong commitment to innovation, tempered by situational reality

- A strong commitment to your followers, tempered by the ability to lead

Above all: maintain a strong personal commitment to your vision.

Practical Illustration

Sarah was nervous about going to see her boss, Robyn, about a request. Robyn was stern, strict, and always carried an air of authority. Sarah lightly knocked on Robyn's door, and she invited Sarah inside.

After some small talk, Sarah cut to the chase. "Robyn, the reason I came to see you today is that I think that our client would benefit from holding our next meeting at a more casual location. I know the rule is that we go to business offices, hotels, and other professional places. However, I could see this particular client being more suited to a casual, friendly dining spot. I think it would have a positive influence on the sale."

Robyn listened and then said, "It looks like you've given this a lot of thought. Follow through with the idea, Sarah."

She was surprised. "Really? Thanks!"

While Robyn was a strict authority figure by nature, she also knew when to be flexible to the rules.

Chapter Ten:
Setting Goals

Good plans shape good decisions. That's why good planning helps to make elusive dreams come true.

Lester R. Bittel

A vision without specific, targeted goals is just a wish or a hope. Without targeted goals, how will you ever know if your vision is being accomplished? A vision needs a project roadmap with milestones, but how do you determine what those goals are? First, we will discuss goals themselves, then how to determine what your goals should be and how to support them.

Setting SMART Goals

SMART goals are:

- **Specific:** The vision itself is general while the goals are specific targets to be met. Specific goals answer the questions of who, what, when, where, why and how questions as specifically as possible.

- **Measurable**: Goals must be measurable in terms of progress and attainment. They must be tracked according to the amount of time or money spent, or results achieved as appropriate.

- **Attainable**: A goal which cannot be met, is not a goal, it is an ideal. If you know you need certain infrastructure in place to accomplish your vision, you should break down your goals into attainable steps you can monitor as each step is put into place.

- **Realistic**: A goal may be attainable, but not with the resources at hand. In that case, you need other goals to build up to the level where the attainable goal becomes realistic. A goal may be possible, but you need the right people with the right amount of time and support to make it happen.

- **Timed**: All goals need to be accomplished within a given time frame. Deadlines may indeed be missed, but without any timetable, there will be no sense of urgency and no reason not to put it off until "later."

Each goal should lead to the "next step" in the overall plan until the ultimate vision is reached.

CREATING A LONG-TERM PLAN

Also called Strategic Planning, the long-term plan is the road map that guides you to the ultimate realization of your vision. As discussed in the previous Chapter. A goal may be possible, but not attainable or realistic – now. You may be missing a quality person for a key position, you may lack the funds, or time to achieve the higher-level goals, so lower level stepping stone goals must be planned.

If your goal is to unify a modern computer network throughout your organization, but you only have a few outdated computers and older shared printers, your ultimate goal will be possible and attainable, but not realistic. If you do not have the money for the new equipment and do not have a strong IT person on staff, your goal will be unattainable. If you need everything done in a week, your goal cannot be timely, as it will take much longer. Intermediate goals, however, can make your ultimate goal realistic, attainable, and timely.

You might first want to increase your revenue through increased sales, a fundraiser, long-term business loan, or by other means. You can make a goal to hire a network guru for a reasonable cost who can analyze your current systems and determine what needs to be upgraded according to modern networking technology. That analysis will provide you the information to set new goals of buying, configuring and implementing the equipment, then adding the infrastructure to network it all together. In the end, the goal that seemed impossible will become a reality, according to your original vision.

CREATING A SUPPORT SYSTEM

Once your goals are established you need a way to ensure they are set into motion. Duties must be assigned and documentation must be established to support and track progress. A Gantt Chart is a great way to track milestones over a period of time. You need to establish the tools necessary to track progress or development as appropriate. These might include a simple checklist for some tasks and complicated advanced software tracking systems for others.

Monitoring and oversight are the keys to achieving all goals.

PRACTICAL ILLUSTRATION

Sophie presented her goals to Thomas, the leader, and she said, "What do you think of the plan that we have laid out?"

Thomas said, "I think that your goal of updating our technology is specific, measurable, attainable, and timed. However, the only thing that is unrealistic about the goal is how much it is going to cost."

Sophie said, "I was hoping that you could help me brainstorm ways to come up with the revenue."

Thomas nodded. "In the past, we've tried new ways of increasing sales to pay for equipment that we needed, or taken out a business loan. But given the time frame, I feel like our best bet is a fundraiser."

They included the fundraiser idea in the final goal, making sure once again that the goal was SMART: specific, measurable, attainable, realistic, and timed.

Closing Thoughts

To be a leader, you must first see yourself as a leader. Based on what you have learned so far, you now know what qualities are important in a leader and you have prioritized them as they apply to you. Experience is the greatest teacher, however, and there is no substitute. If you ever had a boss that infuriated you and made you want to quit your job, you know what not to do. If you ever had a parent, teacher, coach, or supervisor who inspired you, you have a good example to follow.

- **Thucydides:** The bravest are surely those who have the clearest vision of what is before them, glory and danger alike, and yet notwithstanding, go out and meet it.

- **Woodrow Wilson:** The ear of the leader must ring with the voices of the people.

- **Theodore Roosevelt:** The best executive is the one who has sense enough to pick good men to do what he wants done, and self-restraint to keep from meddling with them while they do it.

- **Sun Tzu:** A leader leads by example not by Force